THE NAKED TRUTH OF OWNING A BUSINESS
SECRETS REVEALED BY AN ENTREPRENEUR

BEVERLY MEEKINS

B.A.M Publishing Company
Matteson, Illinois

Copyright @ 2011 by Beverly Meekins

All rights reserved. No part of this book may be reproduced in any form or by any means including electronic, mechanical or photocopying or stored in a retrieval system without permission in writing from the publisher except by a reviewer who may quote brief passages to be included in a review. For permission of use, please contact: info@bampublishingco.com.

This book is designed to provide information in regards to the subject matter covered. It is sold with the understanding that the publisher and the author are not engaged in rendering legal, accounting, psychological or other professional services. If advice or other expert services are required, the services of a professional of your choosing should be sought. While every attempt has been made to provide accurate information, neither the authors nor the publisher can be held accountable for any errors of omission. Any resemblance to actual events or locales or persons, living or dead, is entirely coincidental.

ISBN-13: 978-0-9832359-0-3
LCCN: 2011909877

Editorial Team: Lissa Woodson, Erica Weber, Jeanne Ricks
Cover Design Barron Steward of www.barronsteward.com
Interior Book Design: Lissa Woodson of www.macrompg.com
Interior graphics: Tim Newlin of www.timtim.com

Distributed by:
Ingram Book Group

B.A.M. Publishing Company trade paperback edition May 2011

10 9 8 7 6 5 4 3 2 1

Manufactured and Printed in the United States of America

Dedication

This book is dedicated to my parents,
Grace and William Meekins
For all you have done and continue to do!!!

Acknowledgements

This book has been my 'passion' for several years. But it is only by the grace of God that it has come to fruition. When I set out to write a book, it was my intention to write a work of fiction. In fact, I already had a concept developed. However, it was His decision that I launch my writing career by sharing my observations and experiences about business ownership.

I would like to express my deepest gratitude to Lissa Woodson for her expertise, encouragement, and developmental input. Without her, I might never have finished this book. Thank you to best selling author Naleighna Kai for her input; Barron Steward for the fantastically creative cover design; Ehryck F. Gilmore, CH for introducing me to my "team" and your continued insight as the world's best life coach; Erica Weber for the initial edits; Jeanne Ricks for her much appreciated fine-tuning; Tim Newlin for the wonderful interior artwork, and Belinda Turner for listening patiently to my ideas and diplomatically critiquing every draft.

I would also like to acknowledge Jeannette Carter, Cynethia Keith, and Trina Streeter-Kluka who read many of the drafts; Sheila Boyd, Kimauna Catchings, Carole Meekins, Janice Meekins, Pamela Meekins and Astrid Tompkins, who listened to me drone on and on and on incessantly about this book; and Natalie Chadwell, Lucy Green, Darren McKinnis and Paula Ross for their support and encouragement. Finally, I would like to mention Deidre Blair, the first published author that I had the privilege of personally knowing. Watching her navigate the process inspired me to forge ahead with my own book!

Last but not least, I would like to thank my husband, Byron Powers, for supporting me in everything that I do.

And to the person reading this book, may you find something within these pages that inspires you to forge ahead with your entrepreneurial endeavors or helps you gain a greater appreciation for your current job.

About This Book

Owning a business is a romantic notion for many people. The same goes for those "happily ever after" fairy tales read to us when we were children. Only later did we come to find out that they weren't quite the complete story. The concept of being your own boss, setting your own rules, and making a boatload of cash has put a fire in the hearts of even the most jaded people. Witnessing the success of people who started with nothing and achieved astounding results could be just the springboard example that aspiring business owners could model. We all know the story of Bill Gates who dropped out of Harvard to launch Microsoft. Louise L. Hay, self-published a book that had been rejected by all major publishing houses, only to have that very same book land on the *New York Times* Bestseller's list. She then launched Hay House, which is now a multi-million company with headquarters on every major continent. At the age of 30, Jeff Bezos gave up a lucrative career at a New York investment firm to start Amazon.com in his garage. Madam C. J. Walker was the first female millionaire in history. She made a fortune by developing and marketing beauty and hair care products for Black women before going on to teach and help other women build their own businesses.

Stories like these, and many others in the same vein, can be an inspiration to anyone. But does everyone take into consideration the personal sacrifices that these entrepreneurs made along the way? Are many people aware of those behind the scenes failures and heartbreaking decisions that no one has written about, let alone knows? Have people taken into account their personal drive, determination, and ability to stay the course even when the going was rough and those around them told them to give up?

Owning a business sounds good on paper--as does that whole "until death do us part," thing, but the reality is that many outside variables can make it an uneasy task. Unfortunately, most do not realize that personal variables can be more of a deciding factor. *You* are the business. Your decisions, your actions or inactions: saying 'yes' when 'no' is a better course of action, knowing when to cut something (or someone) loose or scale back: are the major factors that drive the failure or success of a business. When thinking about things from that perspective, owning a business can be as frightening as finding out that your wig has been on backwards all day.

Many business owners enthusiastically proclaim the joys of business ownership; however, most have not always shared the naked truth about the flipside. There's a whole lot more to launching and sustaining a successful business than just choosing a name, a direction, and raking in the dough. In this book, I will share with you what many successful business owners learned the hard way and reveal secrets that everyone should know before embarking on the entrepreneur's yellow brick road.

The information provided within these pages is for those who are considering starting a business but haven't taken the leap just yet. It provides tips, advice, and examples of different challenges that should be considered. Overall, it may force you to take a step back and evaluate whether starting a business is really in your best interest. There is a reason why a large percentage of new businesses fail. Prospective entrepreneurs focus on all the mechanics of starting a business, but many do not adequately assess themselves and determine whether they *really* want to make the sacrifices necessary to own a successful business.

Oprah Winfrey stated so eloquently, "It doesn't matter who you are, where you come from. The ability to triumph begins with you." Yes, it is important to consider the right business structure and understand your chosen industry and competition when starting a business. There are thousands of references and books on these topics, but they don't address the most important one – *you* and how much of yourself you are willing to give to ensure the success of your business. How much are you willing to give of your time, energy, and your life to make it work?

This book is based on knowledge gained from decades of working with entrepreneurs as a consultant and from being an entrepreneur in my own right. I have not conducted focus groups or spent years doing formal research. I will not try to fill your head with statistics and studies. Instead, I used observations from my own experiences and give you the tools to analyze the failings of others. Please don't take offense if you see some of your own personal characteristics discussed in this book. In fact, you should be ecstatic if you are represented in one or more of the case studies. An honest self-evaluation can determine whether you have what it takes *before* spending time, hard-earned money, and mercilessly harassing friends and associates in the process only to later tuck your tail between your legs and waddle up Failure Street.

While all situations outlined in the case studies actually occurred, names, occupations, and minor facts have been altered so that I will still have friends and associates after this book is published. I strategically created profiles from composites of business owners, so no one particular person is represented. That being said, to those who have interacted with me and *think* you recognize yourself; you might be suffering from a touch of narcissism. ☺

People who have visions of becoming a great singer and performer and cannot actually carry a tune even if it came prepackaged and with instructions, might hear the words, "Don't quit your day job," quite often. Sometimes it is enough to make that person rethink their plans and choose another course. Unfortunately for the ears of the unsuspecting public, others have still managed to hit the airwaves. In those times, we can be grateful that there is an off switch to save our sanity. Those of you who have been awake at night pondering whether to make that move, but are reluctant, this book will be useful in evaluating your course of action. It will motivate some to move forward with their business initiative, and for others, it will convince them to "keep their day job."

Whichever road you take, if this book propels you onward and upward or if it prevents you from making a choice that can come back to bite you in the butt…I have accomplished my goal.

"I knew that if I failed I wouldn't regret that, but I knew the one thing I might regret is not trying."
Jeff Bezos, Founder and CEO of Amazon.com

Don't Fall Asleep at Your Resting Place

For most of my professional life, I knew I was destined to start a business. I enjoyed and excelled at several jobs, but always felt like something was missing. I constantly felt inspired to have my own business, but unfortunately, my desire for a steady paycheck and fear of taking a risk prevented me from acting on my passion. Fear is a powerful non-motivator. Fear is the very thing that can keep a person's feet from moving even when a Mack truck is headed in their direction. Fear can make a person succumb to other's visions for their lives instead of forging their own path. Fear can keep a person in a job they absolutely hate, rather than stepping out and choosing another path for their life. Fear can make people settle rather than pursue their passion.

When the corporation where I had worked for more than eleven years was sold, I was crushed. Armed with a hefty severance package, it was the perfect time to launch my own business. Instead, I jumped at what I refer to as a "resting place" job--a position where one gains valuable experience, refines skills, and plans their destiny, but stays deadlocked in a holding pattern instead of coming in for a safe landing. Although I didn't actively pursue this type of job, I was relieved when it came knocking at my door.

A professional associate informed me of an entrepreneur in need of business development assistance. At the time, I was lounging at home, dreaming about launching my business, and enjoying being a housewife. (Yes, people still actually enjoy that job, too!). Even though I relished my break with reality, and not having to brave Chicago temperatures that were cold enough to grow frozen vegetables; I recognized the need to earn an income of some sort, so I arranged to meet with my potential employer. Initially, I interviewed to simply write a strategic plan for business expansion, but by the end of the interview, I had become the Chief Financial Officer (CFO) of the company. Hot damn! She believed in my abilities, and so did I (but not enough to go full steam ahead on my personal agenda). Even though I possessed all the skills, credentials, and experience to sustain a successful CPA business, my phobia of losing a steady paycheck had prevailed yet again. It was the same as having the potential to become a delectable Godiva chocolate and settling for being a store-brand chocolate bar.

Although being a CFO was a great opportunity, it was also very dangerous. Now I would have the "feeling" and responsibility of being an entrepreneur without any of the risks or rewards. The business didn't have a structured financial management system in place which meant that I had to set up an entire accounting department. I toiled year after year, implementing financial systems and creating the "perfect" accounting department and cash flow models. I will admit, it was a bit of an overkill given the size of the company and industry, but I was in my element now. I was "acting" like a business owner while gaining a steady paycheck to boot!

My responsibilities were eventually expanded to include administration. My entrepreneurial juices were flowing so heavily that I handled this new aspect without requiring a pay increase. (No, I hadn't been dipping into the moonshine or indulging in any untoward substances; I was on a delusional high--the worst kind).

Employees routinely solicited my input and advice, basically acknowledging that I ran the day-to-day operations of the company. I was overjoyed and over time, I began to act as though I actually owned the company. I even told the owner that I never wanted to leave and that this was the job from which I wanted to retire. A retirement plan was as non-existent as a raise in the company, so I am sure she found my statement rather hilarious. Later, I wouldn't find it so funny or anything else a laughing matter. While my attitude and behavior were beneficial to the owner, they did little toward helping me reach my dream to own my own business.

Reality set in and the high wore off when I realized the raise that I had been promised on a consistent basis would not hit my hands anytime in the near future. The owner assured me that when the company could "afford" it, I would be compensated for my worth. Yet even when the company *could* afford it, there was always another priority for the owner.

Instead of that pay increase, the owner eventually suggested that I become an *independent contractor* at a substantially reduced rate. Although I'll admit I was somewhat bitter, (okay, a lot bitter), I was grateful for the important lessons I learned during my tenure.

Lesson 1: Don't confuse your 'resting place' job with your destiny.

You should make every effort to excel wherever you work, but you must resist the temptation to confuse it with your destiny. Instead of resting, I fell into a Sleeping Beauty type slumber, and in doing so, delayed all of my dreams while helping another to achieve theirs. Luckily, it didn't take one hundred years or a handsome prince to go through an enchanted forest for me to get a grip on reality.

Lesson 2: *You* have to make your own dreams come true.

You can't wait for someone else to fulfill your dreams and goals. In my case, I exchanged my dream of being a business owner for promised higher compensation. I should have realized that my professional fulfillment was not someone else's responsibility or priority.

And this brings me to my final lesson – *believe what you see, not what you are told.* It doesn't matter how important you think you are, or how much you contribute to your 'resting place' job, there are always clear signs when it is time to move on. My clear sign was that nonexistent raise. I had rested in that place about four years too long. In fact, I was practically in a coma! The words 'independent contractor' and 'at a reduced rate' were the very things that pulled me off life support and brought me back to life.

CASE STUDY 1:

Lenny spent most of her career moving up the corporate ladder. She held a prestigious position in a major corporation and was comfortable with her job. However, her lifelong dream was to be a writer. She had written a manuscript many years ago and received interest from a major publisher. Instead of jumping at the opportunity, she shoved the manuscript aside and continued to work diligently in Corporate America.

One day, she was laid off without an explanation. Instead of seeing this as a blessing in disguise and a chance to follow her life-long dream of writing, she felt as though her world was shattered. Her friends tried to convince her to grab that manuscript and follow her passion, but their efforts were fruitless. Her fear of the unknown surpassed her passion.

Today, her book remains nothing more than a manuscript hidden under a pile of papers and bills. She is still talking about writing a book someday.

Recently, I had the chance to ask Lenny how her husband felt about her pursuing a writing career. She told me that he fully supported her dream. He had even encouraged her to take a year off and see where her writing might lead her. Some writers would give an arm, a leg and a couple of toes for that type of financial and emotional support! I thought for sure she would feel safe in making the decision to move forward. Sadly, though, fear held her back and she returned to what she knew - Corporate America and yet another resting place.

CASE STUDY 2:

Jamie loved the field of medicine and her career as a physician when she first started out. It was clear she was passionate about what she did in the superior evaluations she received from her patients, and the high regard she earned from her peers. Unfortunately, the medical group where she thrived was sold, and the new management focused on volume instead of quality care.

Although her love for practicing medicine remained steady, she detested the new management. Unlike her previous superiors, they did not value her attention to detail, nor her bedside manner. Instead, they wanted her to see as many patients a day as quickly as possible so that they could make the most amount of money. Jamie hated the change, but rather than pursuing a position with another medical group that would have better suited her personality and work ethic, she stayed at a job she hated, and complained about it incessantly.

The medical group was sold over and over again, and with each sale, Jamie's salary declined. Pretty soon, she wasn't only unhappy with her work, superiors and colleagues, but also dissatisfied with the income level. As time went on, Jamie procrastinated in making a change, and instead, fell asleep in a series of 'resting places'. She became complacent with her situation and continued to accept working conditions that were not in line with her belief in how medicine should be practiced. Over time, Jamie began to dislike practicing medicine and became depressed. In her depressed state, she could not muster up the energy to look for another job--or start her own practice.

Eventually, Jamie's employers recognized her lack of motivation and let her go. Today, she is unemployed and living off her savings. More than likely, when her savings dwindle, she will find yet another 'resting place' and the cycle will begin again.

Over the years, I have observed that people's propensity to deal with their current job or situation is easier than stepping out of their box of security and into the land of the risk in order to pursue their passion.

Here are some questions to ponder:

1. Do you recognize yourself in either of the above cases?
2. Are you complacent?
3. Are you allowing fear to hold you back from achieving your dreams and goals?
4. Are you professionally unfulfilled because you are not using all of your skills and talents at your current job?

If you answered "yes" to just one of these questions, then you may be at a 'resting place'. Now is the time to assess yourself, your current situation, and your happiness and determine if you want to hang your hat on a "resting" rack or if you want to put it on, prepare to hit the door and walk toward a destiny that has you in mind.

"Your time is limited, so don't waste it living someone else's life. Don't be trapped by dogma – which is living with the results of other people's thinking..."
--Steve Jobs, CEO of Apple Computer

Don't Confuse Passion with Escaping Discomfort

Don't mistake escaping the discomfort of a poor work environment, boring social life, or bad marriage as passion for a business venture. If you dislike your job so much that you think the alternative is to start your own business, you might be in for a rude awakening. Disliking your job, your boss, your co-workers, your commute, your salary, or anything else in your life is not a good reason to start a business. It may simply mean that you need to launch an aggressive job search, get a divorce or make some new friends instead. It is imperative that you have passion for the business you are considering, or it will simply become another job.

In his book, "The Law of Attraction," life coach and motivational speaker, Ehryck F. Gilmore writes, "Your passion is something that you would do even if you weren't paid to do it." When I read that statement, it resonated with me because I could totally relate and understand.

For over fifteen years, I provided pro bono accounting and business development support for numerous businesses. While I like money as much as the next person, I provided the services primarily because I simply loved the work and enjoyed helping entrepreneurs. I also had a steady paycheck at the time so charging for the services was not the difference between having a four course meal for dinner or serving up bologna sandwiches instead.

While some of the richest and most successful entrepreneurs in the world pursued their passion and climbed to the top; many also demonstrated a desire and willingness to help others. They also made many personal sacrifices to achieve their goals. Keep in mind that if you don't have passion, making it through all of the hard work and long hours that come with opening and maintaining a business will make the process have the look, smell, and feel of yet another resting place.

CASE STUDY 3:

After being laid off from her job, Judy searched months and months for a new opportunity with no luck. When her job hunt did not pan out, she started a real estate business. When that failed, she opened a bookkeeping business. Her final effort was a child care business. When asked, Judy insisted that each business was her 'passion.' And it was--at least for the moment. In reality, Judy clearly had no idea what her passion was. She was always looking for the next "get rich quick" scheme and thought she wanted a business but failed when each attempt proved more difficult than the one before.

Judy hired consultant after consultant in her efforts to start businesses. Her business ideas and vision changed from day to day, and many were not well researched or thought out before money was spent on implementation.

She conducted meeting after meeting about her thoughts and ideas, without successfully executing anything. She seemed to be searching for something in her life and new projects distracted her from what was lacking. The constant pursuit of a new business idea was an effort to fill a void in her life and keep her from focusing on her perceived short-comings.

Judy is now employed in another job that she hates, mostly due to the resentment that all of her business efforts failed. She confused passion for her business ideas with her desire to change elements of her life. She launched a succession of businesses in the hope of getting lucky and ending up with a business she enjoyed instead of taking the time and energy necessary to discover her true passion.

We can equate Judy's actions to a person who is longing to be married. They might know that they have a desire to be wed; but may not have delved into what marriage really is or all the elements it takes to make it work.

Carefully consider the business you want to create:

1. Are you pursuing it because you are truly passionate about it, or for the money or personal gain?
2. Are you simply running from a job or a boss that you hate?
3. Is your mate getting on your last nerve?
4. Are you bored because your children have left the nest?

If you are pondering a business, but have no idea what type of business to start, you probably have not yet discovered your true passion. Alternatively, you may simply be looking for a way out of your current situation. Make sure that the business you are considering is in fact your passion or you might find yourself in the very same position as when you started.

"Passion. The life of an entrepreneur is occasionally exhilarating, and almost always exhausting. Only unbridled passion for the concept is likely to see you through the 17-hour days (month after month) and the painful mistakes that are part and parcel of the start-up process."
--Tom Peters, best selling author

Your Hobby May Not be a Good Business Idea

You might enjoy painting, drawing, sewing, making jewelry, or a myriad other crafts, but it doesn't mean that you will be able to live off your hobby. Some people make the mistake of confusing a hobby for a great business idea. Before taking the leap and starting a business with your hobby as its foundation, consider whether the general public will pay for what you produce. When I say the "general public," I am not talking about your family, friends, and co-workers; I'm talking about complete strangers who have many other alternatives to your product. Once you have an answer, determine whether you will still be passionate about the hobby when it becomes your day-to-day *job*. Making a pair of earrings for family and friends for birthday presents is a whole different animal than making hundreds of pieces of jewelry to lug around to different art fairs or to sell online.

On occasion, I sketch and paint. Although I enjoy this hobby from time to time I won't stay up half the night doing it, nor does the aspect of packing up all my prize pieces to schlep them to one event or the next fill me with a tingle that can't be denied. In fact, I once enrolled in an art class but was so bored with the assignment of painting a fruit bowl over and over that I only lasted two sessions. I am not willing to put in the time to turn my hobby into a business. And I can admit it to myself. Ding! I am now free to move about the entrepreneur's aircraft. Self-evaluation step one is now complete.

People tell me that my sketches are really good and they would love to 'have' one, but none of them ever say they want to 'buy' one. That is a key element--the difference between dream and reality; the art of "hearing" versus listening. They expect to be gifted with one of my many masterpieces. I have not deluded myself into believing that anyone would actually pay me for my artwork. I implore you to be honest with yourself when evaluating whether to convert your hobby to a business.

A person might be willing to stay up all night doing what they love; if you are not one of those people, then it is best to leave the hobby as a hobby. Also, (and this part might hurt)--just because your friends rave about your work, doesn't mean they think it's good enough for you to quit your job and start a business! I hate to admit it, but I have participated in conversations where I rave about someone's craft when I am only buying it because we are friends. But would I purchase enough quantities to sustain that person's life and livelihood? Probably not. One item per person is what I'm good for. I can only hide so many ashtrays or eat so many loaves of zucchini bread. (Well, if it's chocolate chip pecan cookies, then we might be able to negotiate!)

Case Study 4:

Lorraine enjoyed making creative greeting cards. She began by selling them to colleagues for special occasions, and before long, she received orders from businesses and bulk orders for wedding invitations and thank you notes. However, no one ever discussed the bead that fell off here and there or the feather that blew away in the wind when the card was removed from the envelope. The cards were good, but were they good enough for the general public? Not so much. To add insult to injury, Lorraine was a chronic procrastinator and fell behind trying to fulfill even the smallest order.

Based on the perceived success of her card sales to friends and associates, she left a full-time job with the intention of developing a custom card design business. For the first few months, things went well and she was taking more and more orders. However, as time progressed, she was not making enough money to meet her financial obligations. There were not enough hours in the day to create the volume of cards she needed to come close to her previous income. She worked all night but was making little money. It was a fun hobby but very labor intensive as a business. Before long, her hobby was no longer enjoyable. It had become a job, and one that she didn't particularly like. Although making greeting cards was her passion, she was ill-prepared for the challenges involved in transforming it into a business.

Lorraine is now working at another 'resting place' and only makes a few cards each year for herself, her family and very close friends. Her attempt at converting her hobby to a business turned her off to selling her cards to the general public altogether.

Think honestly about your hobby and consider the following:

1. Do you need more skills and training before you are able to consistently create a superior product or service?
2. Is your hobby labor intensive? If so, have you considered whether you will be able to produce it in sufficient quantities at a reasonable cost?
3. Will you be able to fulfill orders in a timely manner?

"The essence of a successful business is really quite simple. It is your ability to offer a product or service that people will pay for at a price sufficiently above your costs...."
--Brian Tracy, self-help author and coach

Use Common Sense When Choosing a Business Idea

A good business idea *for you* is not only one that you know and have a passion for, but one you are willing to find out something about. If you hate numbers, a bookkeeping business makes absolute sense, right? If you can't seem to string a series of sentences together, becoming a public speaker and hitting the circuit is the job for you! Just because you love watching home remodeling shows on television does not mean you can start an interior decorating business without the necessary training.

Several years ago, I facilitated a business planning workshop where I asked each participant to explain their business idea. One participant stated that she was planning to start a business as a consultant coordinator. When I asked her to elaborate, she said she would charge small businesses a fee to introduce them to business consultants, attorneys, and CPAs. My first question: What qualifications did she have to screen these professionals? She did not have an answer. Second question: Do you think a small business would pay for those services? She did not have an answer for that either. I learned that she was not an attorney, CPA, or business consultant, nor did she possess a business degree or have small business experience. Actually, she did not have the appropriate background or experience to provide this service effectively.

In the case above, it was clear that she had not researched similar services already offered for free or at a low cost for new businesses. She didn't take into account that business owners probably wouldn't pay for someone to network on their behalf if they were already strapped for cash. Instead, they were more likely to rely on referrals from friends, family and business associates. Needless to say, as we progressed through the business planning process, she received an eye opening revelation.

There is always the possibility that a business idea that you've devoted a lot of time, energy, and money to might never come to fruition due to circumstances beyond your control. If you are experiencing this right now, take a step back and reflect on whether your business idea is a good one…or not. Again, use common sense. All businesses experience challenges in their beginning stages, but if they are still struggling after many years, more than likely, there is a flaw. Consequently, it may be in your best interest to redirect the energy into something else or as children say when things don't go their way: "take all your toys and go home."

Another indicator of whether or not your business idea has the potential for success is people's reactions when you communicate the prospect to them. If their eyes glaze over because they cannot understand your concept, you may be in denial about the idea and should evaluate it from another angle.

CASE STUDY 5:

For more than fifteen years, Jennifer owned a lucrative business in an industry that was experiencing rapid growth. Yet even with her immense success and hefty salary, she was not satisfied. She wanted to make even more money in order to be well-known among the social elite. She began focusing her attention on the pursuit of a multi-million dollar contract in an area she had no expertise, while ignoring her existing business. For the next five years, she hired a succession of consultants to help her develop marketing materials and business plans for the new multi-million dollar contract that she was certain would land in her lap.

Although these consultants met with her repeatedly, not one of them truly understood what she was trying to accomplish. She shared bits and pieces of her idea, but was unable to properly convey what the big picture was supposed to be. Additionally, Jennifer did not take constructive criticism well, and because her hired consultants knew that, they were unwilling to tell her that her idea was outdated and that she did not possess the right infrastructure or sufficient resources to execute the contract if she received it.

Unfortunately, because Jennifer did not apply common sense to her pursuit, six years, numerous ideas, and tens of thousands of dollars in consulting fees later, that phantom contract is as elusive as finding the perfect man.

Jennifer did not perform any industry research or competitive studies to support her idea. Only then, she might have realized sooner rather than later that her idea was no longer considered state-of-the art and couldn't possibly have taken off the ground. She pursued contracts that her existing business obviously had no ability to implement. Her quest in the promise of money ended up costing her more cash in the long run.

When you're pondering a particular business idea, consider visiting similar or complementary businesses and interviewing their owners about some of the pitfalls that they've encountered. They could potentially warn you about issues that you can find solutions for prior to opening your own doors. You would be amazed at the information you can glean from a simple internet search. Do your research, develop a plan - you will be better off in the long run.

Questions to ponder:

1. Have you prepared a business plan for implementing your ideas?
2. Have you researched the industry? The competition?
3. Do you know your unique selling proposition (what makes you different)?
4. Do you have experience in, or know something about the business that you plan to launch?
5. Do you have, or can you reasonably obtain the human and financial resources to launch the business?

If you answered yes to all of the above questions, then go for it! However, if you answered no to *any* of them, then slow down and do a little planning. Although it's been said that "common sense isn't all that common any more," I beg to differ. You are reading this book trying to get some type of insight, right?

"Most people think it's all about the idea. It's not. Everyone has ideas. The hard part is doing the homework to know if the idea could work in an industry, then doing the preparation to be able to execute on the idea."

--Mark Cubin,
owner of National Basketball Association's Dallas Mavericks

Dream Big…But Be Realistic

We have heard the term "Dream Big" since Moses picked up the twelve commandments. Alright, well maybe that slogan didn't originate so long ago--and I'll admit it was Ten Commandments not twelve. But who knows if "Thou Shalt Not Settle" was one that didn't make the cut? Even the Bible said to "Write the vision and make it plain upon tablets…" if there was one book that gave credence to Dream Big, the Bible gets my vote.

Alexander Graham Bell had a vision that ended up providing the world with a telecommunications system. We would still be using lamps and oil if Thomas Edison had not invented the light bulb. We would all be in danger while traveling from one street to the next if Garrett Morgan had not developed the traffic light. There would be substantially more people in the world if Charles Goodyear hadn't invented a more reliable condom. (Since the rhythm method just wasn't cutting it and those Goodyear Tires could last a long time!) Okay, the last example might be a little drastic, but I wanted to get a key point across: almost everything we use today sprang from someone's idea that was put into action.

Two intrinsic characteristics of most entrepreneurs are that they are dreamers and risk-takers. If they weren't, they would never think of starting a business. However, an entrepreneur must balance those traits with reality. If you can't trust yourself to be honest and realistic, make sure you have a confidante who will be, and who will ask the hard questions. Just because you *feel* passionate about a business idea does not mean that you *should* execute it.

'Dream Big' is a wonderful thought and an even better motivational slogan. In fact, it is better if you have an idea that can lead to great success. However, being realistic means understanding that things don't magically come together. Let's look at a person who wakes up one morning and says, "Honey, grab the kids and let's go to Paris," then sits in the bed waiting for it all to happen. If one has the idea to go on a family vacation, it does take several elements to pull it together--deciding on a place, making reservations, putting the money aside and finally making the trip itself. Oh, and should I mention that if they want to keep their jobs, they will also have to schedule some time off.

Embarking on the journey of starting a business takes planning, resources, support, and a lot of hard work. I have had prospective business owners proclaim, "God told me to start this business." However, the individual had made no preparations for the success of the business. 'Faith without works is dead', meaning you can say it and believe it all day long, but if you don't put some fancy footwork and glad action behind it, nothing will get done.

Noah was told by God to build the Ark. Now I'm sure the first part of his research was, "Well God, that's fine and dandy. But what's an Ark?" The answer laid out specs and details and Noah went to work on building a contraption that no one in that time had ever seen before. Despite the ridicule and probably a few strange looks from his family, he moved forward on Faith and I'm sure some planning. When that first drop of rain was followed by a torrential downpour, I'm certain Noah brushed aside all the hard work and being laughed at as he smiled and said, "Well I'll be gosh darn if He wasn't right!"

But he said it from the interior of his newly built luxury floating zoo and family dwelling, didn't he?

If you are being led to start a business, then it is quite possible that your inner voice is also telling you to listen, learn, and think things through before you launch. I'm all for having higher power, inner voice, or family encouragement pushing people to start a business; but I'm equally sure it means have a proper exit plan before you jump into the lifeboat, while the ship is still perfectly intact.

Although I believe in Divine Intervention and the Law of Attraction, I also believe that there are steps that one must take to reach their destiny or before an idea can be properly executed. I believe that with God all things are possible, but I also believe that He gives everyone the tools and the common sense to apply reason to any approach. If you are purchasing designer suits every weekend and your savings account has only two digits (and that's on the cents side), you may need to come to terms with making a few sacrifices. Donna Karan, Versace, and Louis Vuitton do not need your money. You do! Keep in mind, when the business experiences a cash flow shortage, your workers and bills will still need to be paid, and you cannot pay them in linen, silk or leather!

I have met people who think they want to start a business because they have a friend who has been successful in a particular industry. Because their friend is successful, they believe they will be too. Wrong! Just because a business was successful for someone else, does not mean that launching in that same industry is for you. Additionally, it is important to remember that although it may *seem* as though your friend is making a lot of money, in actuality, they may be living beyond their means to create that perception. Egos are dangerous things and they can have you trying to live a Rolls Royce dream on a Ford Fiesta salary.

The saying goes, "Shoot for the moon, and even if you fail, you'll land among the stars." But even NASA has to plan, test and train for months before propelling our astronauts into space. Take a lesson from the galaxy travelers! Plan first, fly later.

CASE STUDY 6:

John aspired to own a bar. However, he had no savings, college degree, or relevant expertise to support his dream. When his temp job ended, and some of his relatives decided to open a bar, he was enthusiastically on board. Although he had no managerial skills, he decided that he would be the perfect manager, imagining, as most people have, that it would be pretty easy.

Feeling secure in the non-existent managerial position at the still non-existent bar, he declined the temp agency's offer to place him on a new assignment, making him ineligible for unemployment benefits. The group met for months and months planning the new enterprise, yet no progress was ever made.

Sadly, the bar never opened. In all their planning, the group failed to realize that the space where the proposed bar was to be located was in a town that was not issuing any more liquor licenses. It was a critical piece of information that someone with restaurant experience would have learned during the initial planning stages.

Two years later, John had to move back in with his parents. He still has no bar, no college education, and no full-time job.

John should never have turned down work from the temp agency while the business was still in the early planning stages. An old adage states: *A bird in the hand is worth two in the bush.* His actions highlight the mistake that some prospective entrepreneurs make – thinking that a dream can become a reality quickly and easily. Complete your business plan and be thorough. Save enough money to pay your bills while your business is in its infancy stages, and improve your credit score if necessary.

Continue to dream, but do your homework and be realistic.

Questions to ponder:

1. Again, have you completed a business plan?
2. Are you basing your ideas on current information or on something you have been pondering for many years? Could your idea be out of date?
3. Do you know what resources (human, financial, etc.) will be required to launch your business?

"The starting point of great success and achievement has always been the same. It is for you to dream big dreams. There is nothing more important, and nothing that works faster than for you to cast off your own limitations than for you to begin dreaming and fantasizing about the wonderful things that you can become, have, and do."
--Brian Tracy, self-help author and life coach

Don't Quit Your Day Job

Although an entrepreneur must be willing to make sacrifices, some in their zeal to start a business, make *unnecessary* sacrifices. Your business may become successful after you run out and quit your day job, but why do that? Why go through the hassle of hiding your car in your friend's garage because you can't make the car payment? What about having to put your furniture in storage because you couldn't pay your mortgage? Don't quit your day job until everything is in place.

Although there are success stories of people creating multi-million dollar enterprises on a shoestring budget, it is important to remember that they are the *exception* to the rule. It is also imperative to keep in mind that what appears to be an overnight success to you might have in fact been far more complicated, and possibly the fifth, or even fifteenth attempt for that entrepreneur to get their business up and running. What you didn't see was the owner filing for bankruptcy, borrowing from friends and family members, and working multiple jobs just to keep their head above water while they started their business which *eventually* became an "overnight success."

The best advice I can offer is to develop a personal financial plan while you are in the planning stages for your business. The business plan outlines how you will fund your new business and the personal financial plan will help determine how you will pay your bills, feed your family, and put gas in your car if you're not drawing a check from your business. Sit down and map out all of your personal living expenses and don't omit anything. I recommend that you start your budget by listing every expense you currently have. Be realistic; don't prepare a budget based on what you think you should be spending. Don't forget about the five dollar cups of coffee or the magazines that you routinely purchase. Review your bank and credit card statements to ensure that you have an accurate starting point. After you have identified your actual monthly expenses, pare down your budget to determine the bare minimum that you are able to live on. That is the amount that your business will need to pay you if you quit your job. Even if you are generating some revenue from the business, initially, it may not be enough to pay your business expenses *and* your salary.

If you don't have a dime saved and have a poor credit score, you may need to do some preparatory work before quitting your job. It is possible to maintain a full-time job by day, and work towards achieving your entrepreneurial dreams in the evenings or weekends.

If it is at all possible, keep your full-time job while you launch your business so that you have enough money to meet your personal financial obligations. Yes, it might be difficult; yes there might be fourteen plus hour workdays and minimal free time. But you'll still be able to keep your car with a tank of gasoline in it, your house (with furnishings), and put more than just peanut butter and jelly sandwiches on your table.

I know this may be a stretch for some of you, but you should also try your best to pay off all of your bills *before* taking on more debt, something that is inevitable when starting a business.

When I launched my business, I had saved up enough money to meet my personal obligations for several years. I had also saved enough working capital to sustain the business if I did not have a single customer, of if they failed to pay me in a timely manner. I would like to emphasize that my personal financial plan did not include new outfits, vacations, manicures, lobster dinners…you get the picture. Much to my chagrin, I even had to stop incessantly redecorating the house--one of my favorite hobbies. I did without the extras for the first few years. The good news is, that period of my life taught me that I could live with a lot less than I thought I could. And it gave me a greater appreciation when I was able to add in those "extras" when the money was right.

CASE STUDY 7:

Celeste always aspired to start an interior design business. She excelled in design and had the skills needed to launch and sustain a successful business. However, she also enjoyed the finer things in life. Throughout her tenure as a Vice President in Corporate America, she purchased a new BMW every three years; wore only the best designer business suits; and was known for eating at the most luxurious restaurants in the city. She purchased jewelry, handbags, gifts--you name it. To Celeste, her image was everything. When she walked into a room, she wanted to be the center of attention.

Over time, Celeste grew tired of her corporate design position. She longed to start her business. However, her excessive consumption and meager savings made it impossible to leave her job. Furthermore, she was not willing to scale back her spending or give up her evenings and weekends to start the business.

Needless to say, Celeste is still working in Corporate America, with no savings and letting her dream die a little more each year.

Celeste was unwilling to make the sacrifices necessary to save enough money to allow her to either transition to a lower-paying, less-time consuming job, or leave her position altogether in order to focus on her business venture.

Before you quit your day job, consider the following:

1. Is your current job flexible enough to allow you to spend your evenings and weekends working on your business (e.g. not a lot of overtime and weekend work requirements)?
2. Do you have sufficient funds available to pay your personal bills while you are building your business?
3. Do you even know how much money you need to pay your personal bills?
4. Are you willing to spend the majority of your spare time working on your business?
5. Will your family situation allow you to work on your new business evenings and weekends?
6. Do you have a lot of credit card debt?
7. Are you concerned with keeping up with the Jones' or what other people think about your material possessions?
8. Do you impulse shop?

Securing the resources to launch a business takes discipline and sacrifice. If you are not already wealthy, then you may have to give up both time and money to launch and sustain a successful business. If you are unwilling to make those sacrifices, then examine your spending habits *before* undertaking the monumental task of entering the entrepreneur's ring.

It is certainly good to dream big. In fact, it is better if you have an idea that can lead to great success; but don't run out and quit your day job before you have taken a hard look at your life!

"If it really was a no-brainer to make it on your own in business there'd be millions of no-brained, harebrained, and otherwise dubiously brained individuals quitting their day jobs and hanging out their own shingles…"
--Bill Rancic,
winner on Donald Trump's "The Apprentice"

Don't Discount Your Experience

One of the many reasons some potential entrepreneurs do not pursue their passion is that they believe they lack the 'right' education or credentials. However, when evaluating your business idea, you must not focus solely on *your* education and credentials, but your *ability* to execute the plan. And never underestimate the value of your experience. Many times, work experience surpasses what can be learned in a book.

There was once a CEO who said, "I don't have a degree, so I hire people who have them." This means you can develop a team with the right experience and credentials, but must remember to budget for their salaries. However, before you consider paying anyone, you must know the skills and talents that *you* lack. If you decide that more education is in order, your local community college can be your best friend. In my opinion, one of the worst things a potential entrepreneur can do is fail to honestly assess him or herself. The next worst thing is for them to come to the conclusion that they know it all and refuse to pay for good help.

CASE STUDY 8:

Betsy runs a highly successful construction company. When she initially planned for the business, she recognized that she had no experience in the trades or construction. However, she realized that if she enlisted the support of others with the right experience she could successfully launch her business. She had the right affiliations and connections to be considered for lucrative construction contracts.

Recognizing her deficiencies, Betsy partnered with a successful engineer/project manager and together they ventured into the business. Although Betsy knew that the contracts they were bidding on were significant, she was not greedy. She understood that fifty percent of nothing was nothing and that she could not make it work without a partner. She shared the profits with her partner and hired experts in the areas they were lacking. Betsy recognized the value of an accountant and hired a CPA. She also hired a business consultant to brainstorm ideas with. She created a team that could help her ensure that the business would be a success.

Today, Betsy's business is growing and she continues to fairly compensate others for the expertise that she lacks.

If you don't possess the skills and capabilities to execute your business plan successfully, and you aren't interested in obtaining additional education or credentials, make sure you identify individuals to fill in the skill gap. Remember to include reasonable salaries for those individuals in your plan. You may also want to consider providing them with a small portion of ownership in the company if you don't have the resources to adequately compensate them. However, if you choose that route, make sure you read the chapter entitled, "Partner or Prisoner" first. Another alternative for excellent 'free' advice is to select key people for your board of directors. Don't automatically choose friends and family members for your board if you need additional expertise to round out your skills. A solid board can give you serious clout in places where you may lack entré and also fill-in a resume which is lacking. The board should not be wasted with Uncle Bubba or the Bundy's across the street - the board deserves serious consideration.

Before you decide to launch your business, consider the following:

1. Do you possess expertise and/or experience in the business you are interested in launching?
2. Have you performed a self-assessment and determined the skills and capabilities you lack?
3. Do you have access to sufficient resources to pay for the skills and expertise that you lack?
4. Are you *willing* to pay for the skills you lack?

"You can take my business, burn up my building, but give me my people and I'll build the business right back again."
--Henry Ford, founder of Ford Motor Company

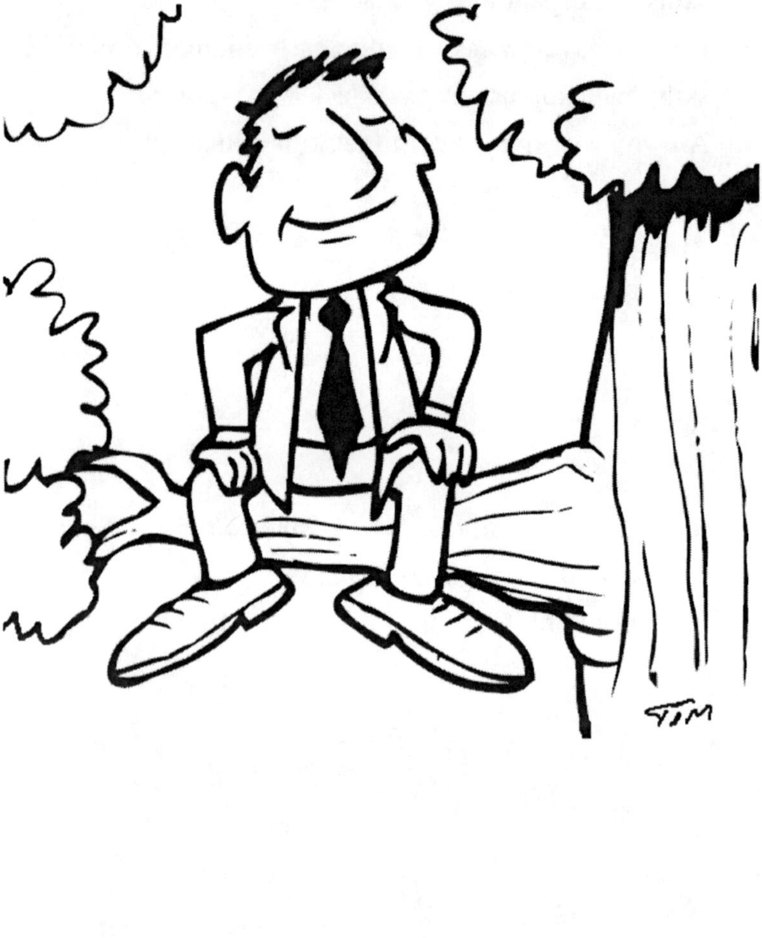
TIM

Don't be a Tree-Dweller

Strategic and broad thinkers rule the world. A person focused on details all of the time can develop an entire business model on the trees, while losing the ability to operate at the forest level. I refer to this type of person as a *tree-dweller.* I believe that tree-dwellers make excellent employees, but not necessarily good business owners. You must be able to see the big picture when you own a business. If you perpetually get caught up in minor details, there won't be any time left to actually run your business and accomplish your main goal – to have a successful venture that earns you a decent income.

CASE STUDY 9:

Francine owned a wholesale distribution business that had the makings for success, yet she found herself struggling. Each day, she was trying to make heads or tails from receipts, while also entering the day's transactions into financial accounting software. While she was at the office, her driver made deliveries to clients across state lines, regardless of how small the order was. Most were usually less than fifty dollars and could be more cost effectively served by using an outside shipping company. She rebuked the idea of requiring a minimum order amount for delivery because she felt that delivery gave her driver the opportunity sell additional merchandise during delivery. However, her driver was on a tight schedule and made only cursory attempts to sell additional products. Francine was so busy focusing on the details of purchasing and delivering product in small increments that she didn't take the time to realize that she was bankrupt on paper and could be shut down any day for failing to remit sales taxes.

To make matters worse, she thought she knew everything. When I informed her that she was entering information incorrectly into her financial software, she insisted that something was wrong with the very popular and widely used software! I also suggested that her time would be better spent on marketing and planning and that she consider the services of a part-time bookkeeper to record her financial transactions. However, she was so detail oriented that she was unable to delegate that task.

Francine's business is now closed, all of her credit cards are maxed out, and her personal credit is ruined.

Alright, let me issue this little disclaimer: I'm not implying that you should not pay close attention to details when you open a business, but as a business owner, sometimes it is more practical and less expensive to hire someone else to perform certain tasks. Attention to detail is valuable. However, if you lose sight of the fact that you are bankrupt on paper because you are so overwhelmed with the details of the day, then you have become a tree-dweller. As a business owner, it is imperative to make sure to always keep your eye on the big picture. You cannot get so caught up in the details, that you do not have the time to analyze your business and move it forward. In my opinion, if all of the day-to-day activities rest with you, then you are creating a job, not a business. A business should be able to run for a few seconds in your absence.

If you have an inkling that you're more likely to dwell in the trees while the forest burns, ask yourself the following:

1. Do you always feel the need to control all aspects of a project or activity, even if others have more expertise?
2. Do you trust others to assist you? Are you able to delegate effectively?
3. Do you consider yourself a strategic thinker or visionary?

"You are surrounded by simple, obvious solutions that can dramatically increase your income, power, influence and success. The problem is, you just don't see them."
--Jay Abraham, Founder & CEO of Abraham Group

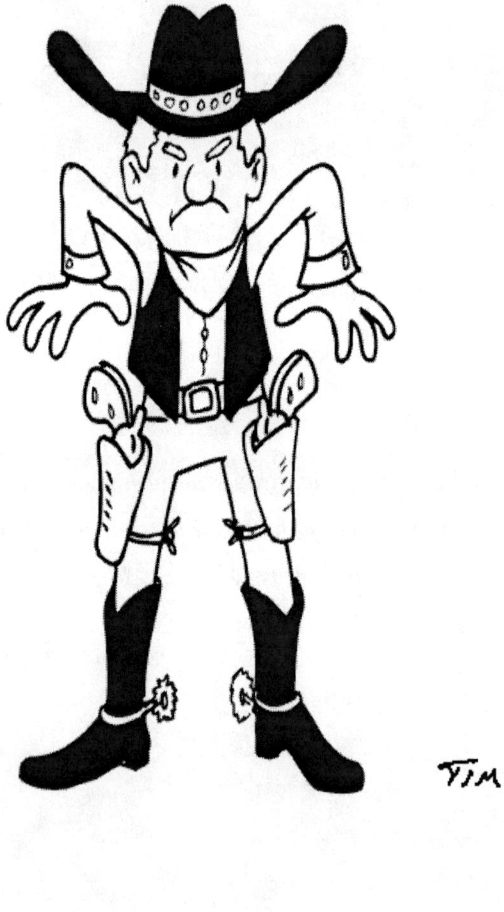
TIM

Maintain Emotional Control

When I started my business, I had no idea how emotionally draining it would be. I knew there would be a lot of hard work and late hours, but I had no idea there would be times, numerous in fact, when I would wonder what I had gotten myself into; question my decision in the first place; and even consider giving up and walking away.

As an employee of a company, there are many things you take for granted without even realizing it. For example, you don't think about how quickly (or slowly) the customers pay their invoices, or whether or not you will get a paycheck that week. You go to work everyday and *assume* that the money is in the bank to pay you. You know that you will get paid regardless of how much time you spend surfing the internet or planning your weekend on company time and dime. However, when you own a business and you are the boss, you *do* worry about those things because now you are responsible for not only yourself, but your employees as well. When the customers don't pay, you still have to pay your employees! They are not going to be content with "your paycheck is in the mail." Said paycheck had better be in their accounts or you may walk in one day to an empty office. One of the first signs a business is in trouble is when employees do not receive a check on time or when their check bounces. The company might also be in a spot if they ask everyone to take a pay cut; but recognize it as an attempt for the company to stay afloat while they figure out which lifeboats to inflate.

Owning a business is not for the weak. You must be emotionally strong to start it and even tougher to effectively run it. In the early years, it is quite possible that you will work harder than you ever did in your life, and get paid less than any other time. You will confront many challenges and must be able to control your emotions at all times. Your staff, vendors, and associates must believe that you are in control, even if you feel as though your whole world is collapsing. When you appear out of control, those around you will lose confidence in your abilities as a business leader and will elect not to do business with or work for you.

In case you are wondering, examples of being out of control are: yelling, screaming, cursing, crying, whining, and indecisiveness--the list could go on. Sometimes on the television show 'The Apprentice', several leaders in the Trump organization sit across the boardroom table with people vying for a top spot within his company. The show is competitive with several people of all ethnic backgrounds and genders and varied stages of education working as a group to complete an array of business-oriented tasks. At times, the leaders at Trump are silent and watch how each person interacts, explains their position or defends themself against attack--and mostly how they go on attack. Most of the winners (excluding the celebrities) end up being people who not only have leadership qualities, but can remain calm under pressure, are articulate and can manage themselves and others.

I am certain that in your career you have encountered the people who believe that being a tyrant is what motivates people to work. I have personally witnessed business leaders who lost many good employees due to their tendency to yell at and patronize their staff, and it can have devastating results. There aren't many secrets in the business community. Word will get around and competent professionals may choose not to be associated with people of that caliber. Furthermore, this type of business owner often fails to consider the significant cost of recruiting, hiring and retraining new employees.

CASE STUDY 10:

Claudia operates a successful business, but the turnover in staff has been bad for morale and for the company overall. She has a bad habit of raising her voice when speaking to professionals. Claudia was often overheard yelling at her employees, husband, and siblings from her large, corner office. Everyone in the office knew to walk on pins and needles around her.

She also shares her personal and financial problems with her staff. Although she drives an expensive luxury car and wears designer clothing, she is never satisfied with her earnings. She constantly complains about not having any retirement savings when it is common knowledge that she receives a five figure paycheck every month that she chooses to spend instead of save. When the company is low on cash flow, she whines to her staff about having to withhold her own paycheck in order to pay them and her other bills.

Although she consistently exhibits unstable behavior, she is still in operation, but unbeknownst to her, she has a reputation for being unstable in the business community. Furthermore, she is unable to hire and keep good staff because her reputation precedes her.

She spends thousands each year retraining new staff to replace the ones that leave. With each departure, valuable knowledge is lost and her staff becomes less and less competent. Also, as her staff departs, customers who respect those staff members go with them or elsewhere. Her business which generated almost ten million dollars in revenues per year is now down to less than three million dollars per year.

The same rule applies to a business owner that applies to employees – keep your personal problems out of the workplace. Also, treat all of your employees with professionalism and respect. When you own a business, you must set an example for the rest of your employees, and the best way to do that is through your actions. Don't think for one moment that your own out of control behavior will remain within the walls of your business offices. Always remember that employees talk. They talk to prospective new hires, they talk to other professionals, and most importantly, they talk to your customers.

If you have a tendency to raise your voice and act in a confrontational manner with family, friends and business associates or if you see yourself in the above case study, then consider the following questions:

1. Do you always have to have the last word, even if you are wrong?
2. Do you openly discuss your personal problems in the workplace?
3. Are you unable to maintain your professionalism in the work environment regardless of the challenges? Do you gossip about your workforce?
4. Do you feel that inspiring and motivating others is not your responsibility?

If you answered yes to some of the questions above, I suggest that you evaluate your ability to lead others. Honestly reflect on how you are perceived in a professional setting. Think about your past performance evaluations, promotions or lack thereof. Were you considered a team player? Did others seek you out for choice assignments? It is not always the *other person*, particularly if there has been a consistent pattern throughout your career.

"If your actions inspire others to dream more, learn more, do more and become more, you are a leader."
--John Quincy Adams, Sixth President of the United States

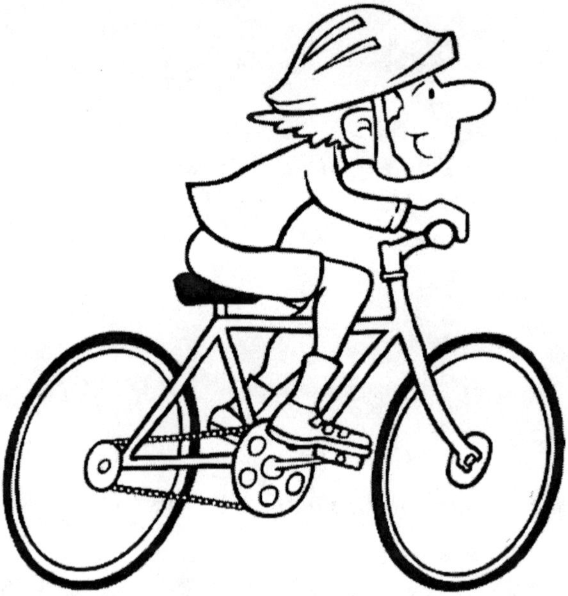

Improve Your Physical Fitness

Starting a successful business is like running a marathon--it takes stamina and perseverance. All day, you run around, marketing and networking, and then spend evenings and weekends actually doing the work such as recording or reviewing transactions, fulfilling orders, preparing correspondence, etc. In the beginning, sick days, holidays, and vacation days disappear faster than a friend who owes you money. If you're not working, you are thinking or worrying about what you should be doing. Initially, you will be the sales person, the secretary, the receptionist, the technician, the *everything*. If you have ever watched a marathon you will see that everyone starts off fast from the gate, but over time some start to drag, others fall out, and a few have to be carted off by the paramedics.

Running the entrepreneurial marathon can be exhausting. I am not implying that if you have a disability or a chronic illness you can't start a business, but I am saying that your illness or disability must be well-managed. For example, I have asthma. When I initially started the business, some of my asthma attacks were the result of poor stress management. It was only when I managed my stress and closely followed my doctor's orders that I got the asthma under control. As a result, I was able to work at a feverish pace without bringing on an attack.

You have to have energy and stamina to plan, launch, operate, and grow a successful business, and the only way to do that is to take care of your mind, body, and spirit.

CASE STUDY 11:

Jason has a successful consulting business that, while small, serves his financial needs. He is an excellent technician and works very hard on behalf of his clients; however, he has several chronic illnesses that he doesn't manage as aggressively and effectively as he should. This alone makes it difficult for him to walk more than a few steps without becoming winded. Furthermore, his illness makes it challenging for him to get around as he has steadily gained weight from stress since he started his business. He is now classified as morbidly obese.

Jason's physical size prevents him from being able to actively market his talents. Fortunately, he still receives word of mouth referrals. However, he is concerned about his low energy and ability to sustain the business long-term. It takes him much longer to complete his work than necessary, and he is constantly behind schedule. He knows that if he does not lose weight in the near future, he will begin to lose clients due to his inability to complete tasks in a timely manner.

Case Study 12:

Charles launched an insurance business in his mid-thirties. He was highly self-motivated and energetic and a rising star in the insurance profession. He was finally making the kind of money he had always dreamed of. Unfortunately, Charles had a massive heart attack at the age of thirty-seven. He died instantly. Charles had not had a checkup in years and was unaware of a serious heart condition that was exacerbated by stress. To make bad matters worse, he was an insurance salesman with no insurance.

Don't make the mistakes that Jason and Charles made. Get a checkup before you start the hardest race you may ever run. If you haven't had a checkup in a while, go to your doctor. If you have a chronic illness, follow your physician's orders. If you feel that your weight is an impediment to your energy level, start an exercise regimen and lose some pounds. I lost forty pounds (and it wasn't because I couldn't feed myself either!). I'm not skinny but I can close suit jackets that I haven't worn since the wagon wheel was invented. If you are lethargic and lack energy, a dietary change may be in order. If you need emotional strength, seek counseling or attend a support group. If you need to gain spiritual strength, practice your religion or find some way to connect with God or the Universe. Whatever your issue, manage it before you take on something that will manage you!

When you are physically, emotionally, and spiritually fit, you will be better able to manage the stress of starting a new business. More than that, you will actually come to enjoy the journey.

Some questions that you should consider are:

1. Do you have a physical or mental condition that you are not managing?
2. Have you had a checkup lately so that you are aware of any issues that need addressing or any physical limitations you must consider?
3. If your physician has put you on a particular plan, are you following his or her orders?
4. Are you often lethargic and lack energy?
5. Do you nurture your spiritual wellness?

You get the picture. Get your act together so that your poor health and well-being are not your business' biggest problem.

"There's no reason to be the richest man in the cemetery. You can't do any business from there."
-- Colonel Sanders,
founder of Kentucky Fried Chicken

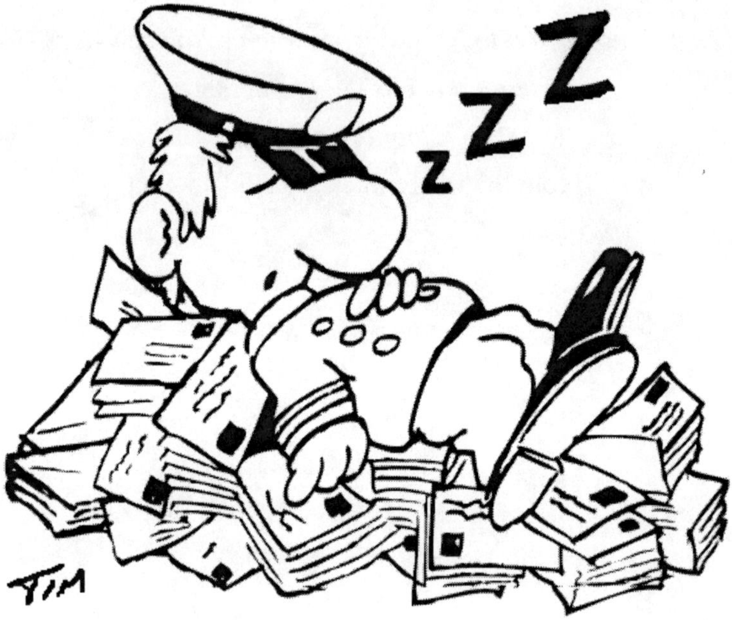
zZZ
TIM

Lazy Employee, Lazy Owner

I believe a lazy employee makes a lazy business owner. If you're the type of person who needs someone looking over your shoulder and micromanaging you in order to be productive, it is likely that you will carry those same unfavorable traits into being a business owner, resulting in an unsuccessful business.

It is a tough thing to do, but be honest with yourself when reflecting on the type of worker you are if you truly hope to succeed. If you do not have a strong work ethic that drives you to excel, I suggest you think long and hard before opening a business. I have yet to meet a *successful* entrepreneur who was not a good employee. If you can't work for others, then others may not want to work for you.

There is nothing more annoying than a boss who spends all day playing solitaire on the computer and conversing with friends on the phone while their employees work hard to keep the business afloat. I realize some of you will argue that you are unproductive at your current job simply because you hate it, but once you have your own business, you will work hard. I don't believe it for a minute. A sound work ethic is not something you turn on and off based on how much you like your job. A good worker is a good worker regardless of the work environment because they take pride in a job well done.

Examine your work ethic. If you goof off when the boss is away;

do everything you can to look like you're working when you're really not; call in "sick" constantly; try to get your co-workers to do your work; leave on time regardless of the status of your assignments; take every one of your breaks exactly on time…you may not be an ideal candidate to start a business.

CASE STUDY 13

Jack supervised a staff of five at his corporate job. He had an undergraduate degree and an MBA so he felt like he deserved to be in senior management. Every day he went to work and delegated all of his assignments to Janet, his best employee. He knew that he didn't have to do anything as long as she was around. He took long lunches and chatted with his friends on Facebook for hours each day.

Jack ultimately decided that he was too educated for his current position and that he would start his own company. That way he would hold the top position and finally call himself the C.E.O. Jack was initially enthusiastic about his company. However, he had underestimated the amount of work it took to start and run a company. Since he was financially secure, he used some of his savings to lure Janet away from his previous employer. Once Janet joined the team, Jack did less and less work until he finally stopped coming to the office at all. Janet got fed up with doing all of the work and begged for her old job back. Jack has since closed the company because he could not find a suitable replacement for Janet and didn't have the work ethic to run the business himself.

While it's a good idea to have a solid leadership team when you launch a new business, that doesn't mean that you can just sit around and be non-productive. While planning your business, think about the type of employee you are or were.

Consider the following questions:

1. Do you take every vacation, sick, and personal day due to you even if you are behind in your work?
2. Do you consistently take long lunches?
3. Do you routinely come in late and leave on time?
4. Do you volunteer to assist your associates when your work is done?
5. If you are a supervisor, do you delegate all of your work so that you don't have to be productive?
6. Do you do just enough to get by?
7. Do you waste time on the internet, Tweeting or on Facebook when you are expected to be working?

Be honest about your work ethic. If you have been a lazy employee for the past fifteen years, it is unlikely that you will be able to muster up enough energy and enthusiasm to be a successful business owner.

"If your thinking is sloppy, your business will be sloppy. If you are disorganized, your business will be disorganized. If you are greedy, your employees will be greedy, giving you less and less of themselves and always asking for more."
--Michael Gerber, author and motivational speaker

Check Your Ego

There is a fine line between being confident and being arrogant. Confidence is vital when starting a business, but if it turns into arrogance, you may find yourself in a bad situation. Arrogance can lead you to *think* you know everything, and rather than seeking other's knowledge and expertise on things you have no experience with, you'll find yourself making decisions that could ultimately be detrimental to your venture's long-term success. When you become arrogant, you are more likely to make decisions that aren't in the best interest of you or your business.

Many of you may remember a famous actor on a major crime series in the 1990's who became a star overnight. After only one season on the show, he decided to leave and make movies. He thought he was a bigger star than he actually was. After struggling for several years, he still had not successfully transitioned from the small screen to the big screen. After years of virtual unemployment, he reappeared on the small screen and is now a more humble television star.

The moral of this story is that a short burst of extreme success does not necessarily translate into long-term success. Just because you were good at a particular job while working for someone else does not mean that you have the skills necessary to run a business. It is important to realize that being *employed* in a particular industry does not necessarily lead to successfully *running a business* in that industry.

Over the years, I have worked with owners of successful Home Health Agencies which were run by superior nurses. Time and time again, I received inquiries from nurses who aspired to open their own agency in hopes of earning more money. From their perspective, they figured that their experience working for a Home Health Agency was sufficient to start one of their own. They forgot that visiting patients and providing quality care did not equate into being an effective business owner who understood marketing, billing and payroll, accounting, regulatory compliance, and case management – all components of being successful in Home Health.

The same holds true for any other type of business. You may be an excellent computer technician, but without sales and marketing experience, time management skills, or effective leadership skills, you may not be successful at owning a technology business. Furthermore, if you don't have the resources to hire the expertise you lack, then you may be in for a rude awakening.

CASE STUDY 14:

George was a computer genius in every sense of the word. He taught himself everything he knew about computers and could find an inexpensive solution to his client's technology issues. He managed networks, built personal computers, and wired telephones – you name it, he did it. The only problem was that George could not explain anything to anyone. The company where he worked had to hire a supervisor to oversee George's work because he could not communicate effectively.

After several years, George decided to start his own technology company. Unfortunately, he had difficulty growing his business because his communication skills did not reflect his technological brilliance. He also had poor time management skills. He never made it to an appointment on time and in most cases was three-to-four hours late. Compounding the problem was that he had no savings and a poor credit score. Therefore he was unable to pay skilled professionals to assist him. George is still trying, but has not yet established a profitable business with a comfortable income due to his communication and time management deficiencies.

Starting and running a successful business is more than just the skills you already have. It's about your ability to sell those skills, attract and retain good employees, lead, inspire and motivate others, fiscal management, and so much more. No matter what you might think, *you alone* are not enough. No matter how smart and educated that you think you are, there is always something that you do not know.

Think about the following before you leap into entrepreneur land:

1. Are you launching the business because it's your passion or because your best friend started one and if she can do it, so can you?
2. Does owning a business appeal to your ego or is it truly your passion?
3. Have you thoroughly researched what it takes to be successful in the business you have chosen?

"Avoid having your ego so close to your position that when your position falls, your ego goes with it."
--Colin Powell, Former U.S. Secretary of State

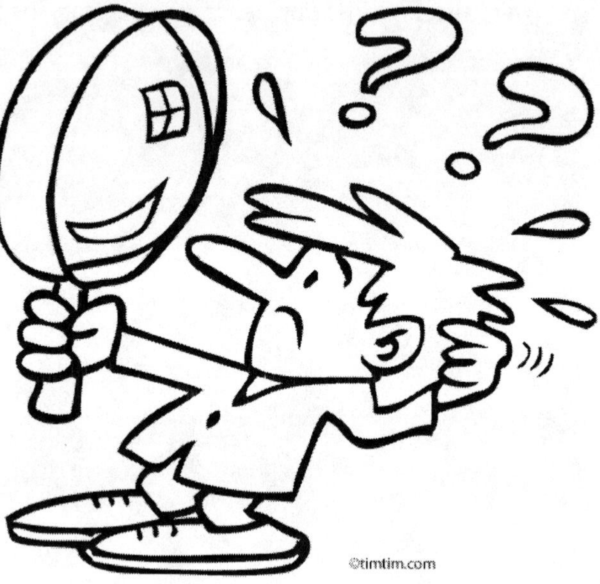
©timtim.com

Low Self Esteem, Lousy Leader

This chapter may seem cruel and even unnecessary to many people, but I have observed the impact of low self-esteem on so many occasions, I would be remiss not to cover this aspect as well. I admit that I am not a psychologist, sociologist, nor do I have any medical or therapy credentials of any kind, however, what I do know is what I have observed.

We have all encountered someone whose low self-esteem led to disastrous personal decisions such as a friend's dating choices. However, self-esteem also plays a major role in business decisions. One day, I was traveling with a business leader to take an important meeting with potential business partners. In the elevator, the Marketing Vice President, whose contact we were meeting, made a harmless comment about the business owner's attire. In my opinion, the comment was both true and a complement but the business owner perceived it as an insult. Several weeks later, the business owner terminated the contract of the Marketing V.P. for dubious reasons. As a result, the potentially lucrative business partnership was called off.

In my opinion, low self-esteem can dramatically cloud business judgment. When I speak with entrepreneurs about why they want to start a business, most recite the appropriate jargon such as I want to help people, or it is my passion, etc. However, some of them started their businesses to make themselves feel or seem important. Some even maintain businesses that are not properly managed or prosperous because they believe that being a business owner gives them status.

Even if the reason you want to start a business has nothing to do with your self-esteem, if you have low self-esteem, you may make a lousy leader. Often, individuals with low self-esteem think everything is directed *at* them and happening *to* them on a personal level, not the business. They make decisions about hiring and firing staff based on their perceptions, which are usually exaggerated due to their own issues.

A successful business leader has to make well thought out decisions based on the business, not their personal feelings of inadequacy. I have also witnessed business owners who terminated good contractors or employees because of presumed insults. Typically when this happens, the business owner will never admit that their decision had anything to do with their self-esteem. They may not even realize it, but you can bet that their employees detected it.

CASE STUDY 15:

Tracy had a successful business. However, several years ago, she terminated her leadership team because she felt they were 'taking over her company.' Since that decision, the business has experienced consistent decreases in revenues and many avoidable challenges due to missed deadlines and poor business decisions. Her employees recognized the negative impact the termination of the leadership team had on the business. However, Tracy constantly states that she is the "president" and "in-charge" and that she is smart enough to take care of everything.

Tracy's low self-esteem led her to feel threatened by the success of her leadership team instead of applauding herself for having the business acumen to select the right people to do the job. Her decision to eliminate that perceived threat led to disastrous results for her business.

It is not my intention to imply that people with low self-esteem should not start a business. What is important is to realize and acknowledge personal issues and compensate for them. You must develop a thick skin to run a business. Sometimes you have to defer to others with more experience and expertise. You have to be able to admit when you are wrong! Women make jokes all the time about men who will not stop and ask for directions. This is not always a laughing matter since the women, who are also in the car, are lost right along with them.

If you are easily insulted, don't like to listen to the advice of others, are reluctant to admit making a mistake, then these traits certainly bear consideration before you hit the planning stages. Nothing unravels a business faster than a dictator in the driver's seat.

Carefully evaluate your personality to determine the impact it could have on your decisions and your business.

1. Do you *always* seek reassurance of others regarding your decisions?
2. Are you constantly asking questions that practically beg for compliments?
3. Do you *frequently* comment on the looks, clothing and superficial qualities of others?
4. Do you hate to admit when you are wrong?

If you have low self esteem, you probably already know it. There is no reason for every one else to detect it through your actions!

"When you undervalue who you are, the world will undervalue what you do and vice versa."
--Suze Orman, personal finance expert and host

Know Your Leadership Style

We have all heard employers say, "Our people are our greatest asset." Although many companies say that and fail to act accordingly, it is a true statement even for the small business owner. If you don't believe that your staff will be equally and, in some cases more important to the business than you, then you need to create yourself an independent contractor job and be done with the thought of owning a business.

Employees who are happy will excel at their jobs, making your overall business more successful. An employee's happiness largely depends on how you communicate with them, how you compensate them, and how you treat them on a daily basis. Employees do not respect leaders who yell, demean others, are condescending, or take advantage of others. Employees are also leery of employers who perpetually "reorganize" as a way to fire good co-workers. It is important you know your leadership style and make adjustments accordingly.

Another important lesson to remember is that your employees are your employees first, associates second, and *possibly* friends third. Although you might have an excellent working relationship, starting a business by treating your employees like close friends will be a huge mistake. They must respect you and your decisions, and in order to do that, they need to view you as their leader, not the person with whom they share the latest gossip. I like to hear a tidbit of gossip here and there like the next person, however, a business owner should never, ever gossip about one employee to another. This rule applies to both *current* and *past* employees. A business owner should not talk about confidential information to other employees. If confidentiality is not maintained, then the employees will not respect you. Also, be cautious about who you share employee information and issues with. The small business community is smaller than you might think. I can't count the number of times I have met someone who knows something about a person that I am acquainted with. You never know who is listening to your conversations and forming an opinion of you based on what you say about your employees. If you constantly tell others that your employees are lazy and incompetent and are ruining your business, what does that say about you?

Your leadership style must:

- exude confidence, not arrogance;
- emphasize your goals and objectives without demeaning others;
- be firm and decisive, without being combative; and
- facilitate a professional work environment without stifling creativity.

Some of the greatest leaders in the world started with a scant few employees and blossomed into powerhouse companies (e.g. Microsoft, Apple, Amazon.com, Google).

Case Study 16:

Georgette owned a small business that employed an office staff of ten. In the span of less than ten years, more than fifty employees had resigned or been terminated for various inappropriate reasons. Past employees conveyed their perceived mistreatment to prospective and current employees which fostered discontent and a poor work environment.

She was driven by greed and personal gain and did not appreciate or care about her employees. Georgette painted an exciting picture of a job while interviewing prospective employees, only to dramatically change the job immediately after they accepted her employment offer. She moved her family members into positions of power and authority, even when they lacked the skills to perform. Georgette was a know-it-all who did not accept the fact that the way she treated her staff was partially to blame for why she always lost her best employees to competitors. Every other year, she used the term "restructuring" to lay off employees and replace them with friends and family members. She also had the inconsiderate habit of saying "It's not personal, it's business" to employees who were being terminated.

Her once successful business declined dramatically to the point that she talked openly about selling it. Many employees only stayed in her employ for as long as it took to find another job.

Georgette failed to understand that her treatment of her employees was a reflection of her as a business leader. When starting and running a business, employees will judge you and the company by how you treat them. If you already have a business and find that you have a high turnover rate, reflect on your leadership style and see if there is something *you* need to change. Likewise, if you are currently employed and are thinking about starting a business and consistently have problems working in a team or no one wants to report to or work with you, don't assume that it is always the "other" person.

Things to ponder:

1. Are you the type of person who has to have everything your way?
2. Do you attentively consider the ideas and recommendations of others?
3. Do you raise your voice when communicating with others?
4. Have you had difficulty working with others on many of your jobs?
5. Have you been terminated from jobs because of the way you treat others in the workplace?

There are numerous types of management styles and volumes of resources on the topic. Do some self-examination and determine whether you are an autocratic or participative manager; do you prefer to build a consensus with your team or dictate to them. It is also equally important that you objectively assess your management strengths. It is important that you know what type of leader you are and how your management style could negatively or positively impact the success of your business.

"A good leader inspires people to have confidence in the leader; a great leader inspires people to have confidence in themselves."
-- Unknown

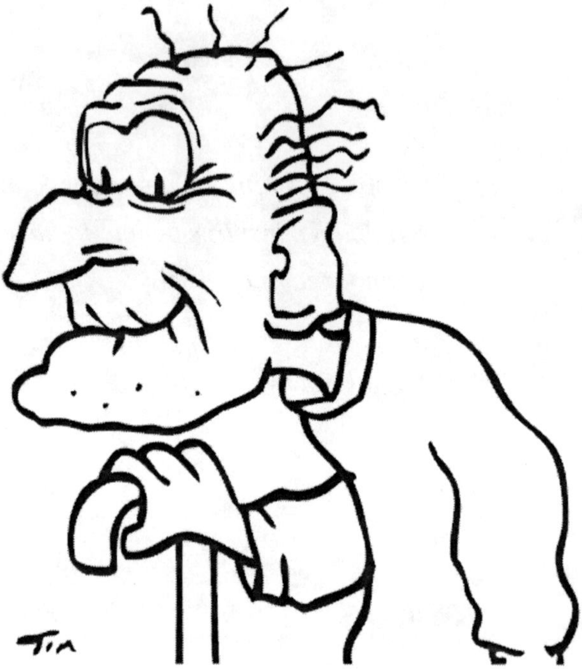

You're Never Too Old

Earlier, I wrote about being emotionally and physically strong to start a business, but that doesn't equate to being a teenager. If you have the energy and the resources to start a business, age means absolutely nothing. If, however, you are starting a business when you're older, it is imperative to incorporate succession planning early in the business development process. I am not trying to be morbid, but it is a fact that if you start a business in your sixties, you many only be around to nurture and run it for twenty years or so. Identify and mentor someone younger who will be able to carry on the business after you. Who knows, you may decide to finally retire at 95!

Case Study 17:

When Harriet's husband passed away, she was forced to take over his business. While she was very capable of running it, it was not her passion. After some time had passed, she took a step back and assessed herself and her capabilities and decided to sell her husband's business. Recognizing that she was not ready to retire at the age of 64, she invested her retirement savings in a franchise. Within ten years, the franchise was a multi-million dollar enterprise.

However, Harriet knew that she needed to consider how her business could be sustained after her death. She developed a plan that included selling and granting shares of stock to her much younger operations manager. Her estate was structured to facilitate a smooth transition, ensuring that her heirs would not be forced to sell the business. In fact, her astute planning included a provision that would allow her children to receive an income from the business for many years.

Harriet recognized that as she matured, she would need to scale back her day-to-day responsibilities. Although she had children, she knew that they were not interested in running the business. Therefore, she rightfully sold shares of stock to a loyal and capable employee. Her forethought secured the continuity of the business after her retirement or death.

In your succession planning, don't assume that your children are willing or capable of accepting the leadership role in your business. In my experience, children are often uninterested and have their own dreams and passions, and may not even have the skills necessary to take on a leadership position in a company they did not create. Make sure your child is interested in the business first, and also has the proper education and training to step into your shoes if they choose to succeed you.

CASE STUDY 18:

Jordan ran a profitable health care company and for as long as he could remember, his vision was that his daughter would join him. He was undaunted when she selected a major in college unrelated to health care. Even when she accepted a position at a company in her chosen profession upon graduation, he still thought she would want to succeed him in the family business one day.

It was a well-known fact that Jordan spoiled his daughter, making her exceptionally difficult to get along with. Within several weeks of starting her job she complained about everything, from her supervisor to her schedule. As was his practice, Jordan rescued his daughter by making her a vice president in his business.

Over time, many key employees at Jordan's company began to dislike his daughter. Even though he knew she was difficult to get along with and possessed poor customer service skills, he made everyone in the office report to her. One by one, long-standing, loyal employees resigned. After a few short years of having his daughter working for him, Jordan's company, which took him years to build, was in total disarray.

Finally, he opened his eyes and realized his daughter was the problem, but he still did not want to take away her salary. Instead, he hired others to compensate for her weaknesses and kept her in the position of vice president with less responsibility than before. He knew that at some point he would still need to find someone to take over his business when he retired, but decided to worry about that later.

Jordan eventually became too sick to run the business. His daughter again assumed a leadership role. Eventually, the business deteriorated to the point that it had to be sold to a more capable competitor. Jordan's daughter is now working for someone else at a salary less than half of what her father was paying her.

Jordan made the mistake that many entrepreneurs make – he wanted his child to succeed him but did nothing to groom her for the position. He was also blind to her poor leadership skills and overall lack of interest in his business. Allowing her to remain in a position without contributing to the success of the company negatively impacted his ability to hire and retain talented professionals. Furthermore, compensating her significantly more than her skills and education warranted proved detrimental when she was forced to get another job.

If you are starting your business late in life, honestly ponder the answers to the following:

1. Do you want to consider a younger partner who can succeed you?
2. Have your children expressed any interest in your business?
3. Do your children have what it takes to assume the leadership role in your company when you step down?
4. Have you started your estate planning?

*"Age is an issue of mind over matter,
if you don't mind it doesn't matter."*
--Mark Twain, author

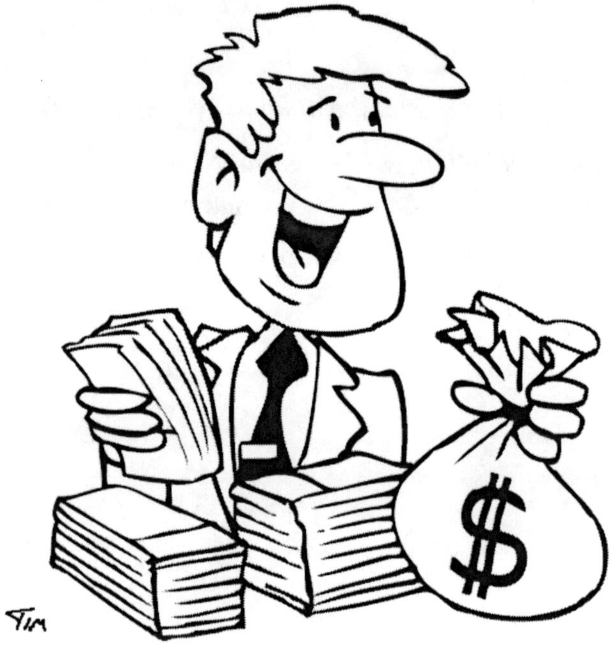

You May Not Be the Highest Paid

This chapter may come as a surprise, but will impart one key fact: you may not be the highest paid in your own business. During the first few years, expect to work the hardest and be paid the least. It is important that you realize this fact *beforehand*, because too often, start-up owners make the mistake of thinking that they will be taking home the largest paycheck -- ("taking their cut off the top!") This misperception could negatively impact the ability to effectively grow your business. You may have the dream, the passion, and the vision, but that does not mean that the money will be so plentiful that you'll need a moving van to help you haul it away.

When hiring personnel, naturally, you will want the best professionals that money can buy. That means that you will have to offer a competitive rate of pay. If you are under the belief that you should make more money than all of your employees, you may not leave enough resources to hire the most competent people. Understand that you are the only one who is willing to work *for free*! It is unrealistic to expect someone to work as hard on realizing your dream as you do without proper compensation, or for significantly less than their market value. Remember it is *your* dream, not theirs.

CASE STUDY 19:

Jackson had a stable business that had experienced consistent annual growth. He earned a six-figure salary and was able to provide his family a comfortable, upper middle class lifestyle. Over the years, he had retained a highly skilled management team that was able to run the business in his absence. He paid each of them a good salary and was able to vacation and pursue other interests as his presence was not required in the office. He led a relatively stress-free life.

After giving it some thought, Jackson decided that he wanted more money. In order to get more for himself, he converted Katrina, a key member of his leadership team, to part-time status and paid himself the difference. Operations ran smoothly for a few months. However, as time progressed, it became apparent that Katrina had been responsible for more functions than he realized. Key tasks fell through the cracks and Jackson realized that he needed to re-hire Katrina on a full time basis. Unfortunately for him, Katrina enjoyed her new part time status and was making more money working with her own clients on the days she did not work for him. When Jackson pushed too hard for her to return to full time status, she resigned the part time position and opened her own business.

About a year later, the remaining members of his leadership team resigned to pursue other opportunities. Although Jackson had a higher income, he was now forced to work in the office regularly. His stress-free existence was a distant memory. Without his talented leadership team, the business suffered and the reputation of the company diminished. Ultimately, he sold the company for less than he felt it was worth.

Jackson didn't realize the full value of his leadership team because he was too distant from daily operations to actually understand their contributions. The decision to reduce the time of one leadership team member disrupted the efficient functioning of the entire team and placed a larger burden on the other members.

The remaining employees of the company who had come to depend on the leadership team were shocked and upset about Jackson's decision. Because he had made the change 'out of the blue', none of them felt they had any job security. Over time, the best employees resigned. One selfish decision to increase his pay wreaked havoc on a previously efficient operation.

As you are planning your business consider the following:

1. Do you think that you should be the highest paid in the company just because you are the owner?
2. Are you willing to lead by example by working hard?
3. Are you willing to perform any function in your business to ensure its success?

Remember, it is important to have loyal, dedicated employees. You should be able to count on yourself to work hard, but you have to recognize the importance of your employees and treat them accordingly if you expect them to "have your back."

"True leadership must be for the benefit of the followers, not the enrichment of the leaders."
--Robert Townsend, Film director, actor, writer, producer

Don't Assume You Will Get a Business Loan

Some prospective business owners think they can write a business plan, go to a bank, and voila...a business loan! Not True. Although I am not a banker and have never had meaningful employment in a bank, I have written many business plans for entrepreneurs who thought that a well-written business plan would automatically result in a loan. I have written them for multi-million dollar businesses and for small businesses. The end result has been the same. The ability to get a business loan for a small or emerging business (particularly service businesses) is generally tied directly to personal creditworthiness. Therefore, if you are planning a business that will require start-up capital beyond what you have saved or can solicit from family or friends, my best advice to you is to maintain impeccable personal credit and savings.

If your credit score is already messed up and there's not enough time in this lifetime to save the money you need to launch your business, you may need to consider more creative ways to secure start-up capital. An option that was previously mentioned is to grant shares of stock to prospective employees in lieu of compensation. Another option is to barter services with other professionals. For example, if you are a technology professional you can provide free web design services to an accountant in exchange for their services. Depending on the type of business you are considering, you may even need to find an angel investor or a venture capitalist; options that will require a lot of research, negotiation and commitment to your vision.

CASE STUDY 20:

Francis had been running a successful service business for almost twenty years when she decided to open a new business. Naturally, she prepared a detailed, well thought out business plan in order to get a loan for this new enterprise. While running her current business, she wasn't great at paying her personal bills on time. She had the money to pay them; but had a habit of throwing her bills in a pile until she could get to them.

After she completed the business plan, she assumed she could present it to her current banker and get a loan for her new business. However, her banker informed her that her credit score was too low to qualify for a business loan. He further notified her that even though her existing business was profitable, it could not be the basis for obtaining a loan.

After being denied the loan, she hastily moved her business account to another bank with the expectation that they would lend her the funds. She was disappointed when that bank also denied her loan due to her poor credit score.

Francis' experience is not uncommon. Small service businesses will not find it easy to get a business loan, particularly if the owner has unsatisfactory credit. Your credit score is your financial track record. If you haven't been diligent in paying your bills, your creditors have three agencies that can help spread the word to other credit grantors: Transunion, Equifax and Experian. If you are thinking about starting a business, it is important that you maintain a good credit score and build personal wealth so you have assets on your personal balance sheet. Do your homework, talk to a business banker before you launch your business. Learn what an acceptable credit score is and what you will need to qualify for a loan.

Things to ponder:

1. Do you know your personal credit score?
2. Do you have personal borrowing capacity?
3. Do you know the requirements for a business loan?
4. Have you met with prospective bankers to determine which bank will best serve the needs of your business?
5. Do you have personal funds to invest in your business?

"The surest way to establish your credit is to work yourself into the position of not needing any."

--Maurice Switzer, Professor and author

Share Your Dreams with Your Family

When thinking about starting a business, it is important that you share your dreams with your trusted family and friends so that they can offer the emotional support that is imperative during the journey toward success. Your loved ones will not only provide support and encouragement, but will also be the voice of reason. I'd like to add a word of caution here and reiterate the word 'trusted'. Not all family members or friends are supportive -- and some may be downright competitive or selfishly not wish to see you get ahead. Make sure you are sharing with someone who has your best interest in mind.

My family and friends were very supportive. If it had not been for my husband's support of my vision and dream, I would never have been able to start and sustain my business. He sacrificed meals, conversation, and companionship while I slaved away in my home office. He also served as the person who gave me a reality check when my thoughts occasionally veered off track. Yes, even I made mistakes and needed to be reigned in!

CASE STUDY 21:

Early in my career, I had acquaintances who were managers and partners in public accounting firms. One particular manager, who was on the fast track to partnership, was in the midst of a messy divorce. I was perplexed by this because he and his wife were upwardly mobile and seemed to enjoy "the good life." I later learned that he had made the abrupt decision to resign from the CPA firm and start his own practice. He figured that if he had to work so hard, he would do it for himself. However, he neglected to inform his wife of fifteen years. If he had communicated his desire to quit his job in order to start his own business, he would have learned that his wife had no desire to struggle to support their family on her own income while he launched this dream. Had he spoken with her first, their marriage might have remained intact.

I'm not naive enough to think that the business was the only reason for the divorce in the case above. However, the *stress* of starting a business at that stage in their married life was the breaking point. Starting a business requires not only financial obligations, but also emotional obligations. Do not underestimate the impact it will have on your family. When you open a business, you are married to your business and your clients get more time with you than your family.

Be fair to your spouse or significant other by communicating openly and honestly with them so that they can fully understand what they are in store for. You will have enough issues to contend with, and it will only make things more difficult without the backing of your family. Make sure they fully understand the sacrifices required. If you are married and plan to remain with your current spouse, he or she must be on board with your plans.

If you are single and embarking on this journey, try not to choose a needy, clingy partner. You will not have enough time to dedicate to the relationship in the early years. As I mentioned earlier, when you start a business, you are married to your business; and sometimes the business can be one jealous brat.

Ask yourself the following:

1. Have you communicated with your partner your goals for starting a business? If not, why not?
2. Is your significant other supportive of your plans? Do they know the 'real deal' not just the positives?
3. How will your new business impact your personal responsibilities to your family and friends?
4. Is your partner aware of the sacrifices he or she must make?

When asked what her greatest challenge was in starting a business, Lilian Vernon, founder, chairman and CEO of Lillian Vernon Corporation replied:

"Staying alive as a business, staying ahead of the game, and melding my business life with my personal life."

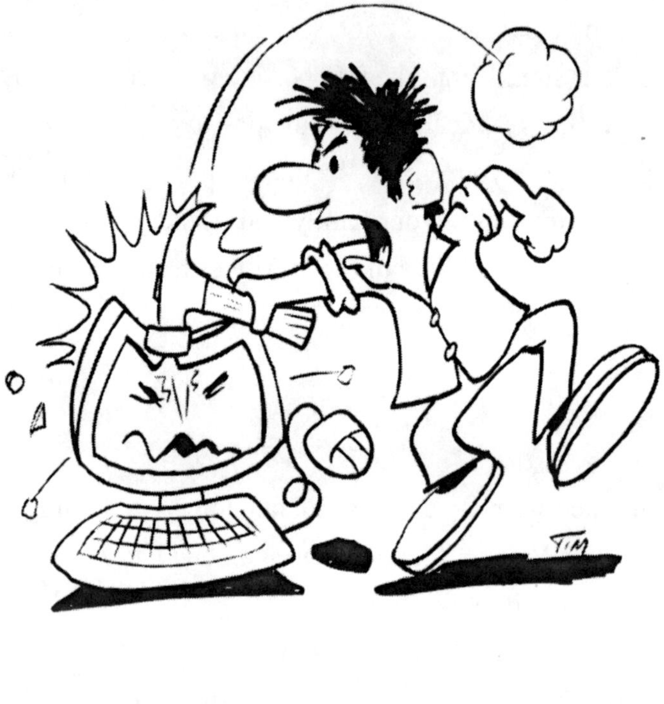

Don't Hire Hacks

It never ceases to amaze me how often small business owners will find a place in their company for friends and relatives who are what I refer to as "hacks." You hire experts; not a cast of characters who show up and *attempt* to do a particular job. Consultants are not hired because they have a sob story, attend your church or are a member of your social club. They are supposed to provide their expertise, not just fill an empty chair. A consultant should not be hired because he is your childhood friend who is down on his luck and out of a job. A good business associate is not necessarily some politician who gives you a string of "alleged connections." A consultant should have the tools to get the job done (i.e. a computer, software).

Think about the friend or relative who told you they could fix your computer, but when they finished, the hard drive crashed and you still had to call a professional to fix the original problem *and* the new problem. There's a difference between *tinkering* with computers and *knowing* computers. Another popular one is, "I can do your taxes!" You had Cousin Bob do them ("the hook up"), and before you could bat an eyelash, you're sitting across the table from an IRS agent with an "intent to levy" notice in your hands. *Doing* taxes and *knowing* taxes are two different things. And all it would take is seeing your precious belongings being auctioned off to bring that point home.

Insufficient cash flow makes some small business owners more susceptible to hiring a hack. But in planning your business, keep in mind that in the long run, it is generally less expensive to spend a little bit more money on an esteemed professional than trying to save a buck for the moment.

CASE STUDY 22:

Jane wanted to create a 501(c) 3 organization to provide housing for individuals with brain injuries. She incorporated the name and hired a family member to prepare and submit the appropriate paperwork to the IRS. Although she had solicited assistance from an experienced attorney, her uncle assured her that he could complete the paperwork for half the price. Every time her uncle submitted it, the IRS rejected the paperwork because there was always something missing. The third time, she was finally successful.

You might think that the third time was the charm, but in reality, Jane finally hired someone who charged the market rate, but knew what they were doing the first time they submitted the paperwork. Ultimately, Jane spent 50% more than she would have if she had used the professional in the first place.

* * *

Penny started her business over twenty years ago, and although it is successful now, that wasn't always the case. In the beginning, she knew nothing about the financial side of running a business, so she paid her sister who was a bookkeeper a small sum of money to act as her CFO.

Penny confidently forwarded all the IRS correspondence she received to her sister to resolve. Five years later, she almost lost her business because her "hack" sister had not responded to any IRS correspondence. Fast forward another five years, and Penny hired a new CPA who helped save the business. It ended up costing her a significant amount of money to resolve the IRS issues after her sister had ignored them for so long.

When you consider launching a business, think about the financing aspects of things, which includes being able to pay the right people to do a particular job well. When you are listening to the sob story of a friend or family member and are considering hiring them, ask yourself the following:

Have you applied the same hiring criteria to that person that you would apply to a complete stranger? Such as:

1. Do they really possess the skills and capabilities you are seeking?
2. Do they have references from their previous employer?
3. Have you developed a detailed job description for the position to enable you to better assess their capability?
4. Would you hire them if they weren't a friend or family member?

If you answered 'no' to the above, then consider giving them a loan instead of a job. With a loan, your only risk is that they probably won't be able to pay you back; with a job, you are risking your business.

"The employer generally gets the employees he deserves."
--J. Paul Getty, founder of Getty Oil Company

Partnership or Prisoner?

Over the years, many prospective business owners have approached me with plans to start a business in partnership with a friend or relative. Often, the decision to partner is made for an emotional reason instead of a business reason. For example, most individuals will not admit it, but the desire to partner often stems from the fear of going at it alone. There is security in taking a leap of faith into the unknown with another person. In other words, if I'm jumping off the cliff, at least I have company.

Launching a business with a partner is not always the best decision. Although you could end-up with a great partnership, you could just as easily end-up in a situation where you feel as though you are a prisoner to the ethics and behaviors of another which aren't in-line with your own. When you are deciding whether or not to partner with someone think of it as a marriage, without benefits. Like a marriage, you must consider if the partner has a track record of success, if they are reliable, loyal, as well as, their personal values and creditworthiness.

If you are a person who values a fancy office with all the trimmings, but your prospective partner is frugal and would like to start off with cubicles, you might already have a problem. If you value financial security and savings, but your proposed partner is a risk-taker who thinks only of today, then you are in for a tough ride. If your credit score is an outstanding 800, but your proposed partner's is only a mediocre 575, you have a major issue that goes beyond a simple personality clash. There are myriad reasons why you should partner with someone, but there are also just as many, possibly more, why you should not. Take the time to write down the pros and cons.

When a business partnership is well thought out and planned, it can be a great idea, but if it is based on fear, friendship, family, or emotions, it can be the exact opposite. Just like any relationship, a partnership requires a lot of hard work and energy. Naturally, there will be disagreements and disputes – sometimes these disputes will be a healthy exchange of ideas, but if you entered into the partnership for the wrong reasons, the disputes are often about power and control. Those two elements can dismantle a business faster than failing to pay your payroll taxes (at least with the payroll taxes you can work with the IRS to resolve the matter).

The most important advice I can give is to view your partnership solely as a business arrangement and remove all emotion. It doesn't matter how long or how well you *think* you know your prospective partner; think about the fact that you might have to spend the rest of your life interacting with them more than you do with your own family. I recommend that each partner provide the other(s) with verification of credentials and a current credit report. Develop an operating agreement that includes an exit strategy so that if one of you decides to discontinue the relationship, the business remains steady and successful. Hire a good attorney to make sure that everything is fair and favorable.

Excellent communication skills are critical for a partnership to be successful. You must be on the same page regarding the vision, strategy and expansion plans, financial management, and the staffing of your joint venture. Be proactive in discussing your goals and expectations with your partner.

I cannot stress how important it is that you know in advance your partner's financial past and present, as well as how they manage their money and debt. It is a good indication of how they will approach the business.

CASE STUDY 23:

Melody opened her medical practice on the best side of town where it flourished successfully for more than fifteen years. Her cousin Lucy, also a physician, had her own practice, but on another side of town. Their clientele were vastly different. In an attempt to grow both of their practices and split costs, they decided to go into partnership together.

On the surface, it sounded like a logical arrangement; however, if they had asked each other some simple questions, they would have learned that their values were very different, making it a bad idea to go into a joint venture together.

Lucy had bad credit as well as outstanding tax liens; while Melody paid her bills on time and had excellent credit. Additionally,

Lucy had a rigid and stern management style and personality; while Melody liked to build consensus and positive relationships. Lastly, Lucy liked black and chrome furnishings while Melody favored a spa like atmosphere with tranquil colors.

Instead of outlining their business arrangement in a legal document before venturing into their partnership, they spent most of their time searching for the right office location and deciding what medical management system they preferred. Melody placed all of the utilities in her name thinking that Lucy would automatically know that she was required to pay half. Soon they struggled to communicate effectively about the most minor details and were always involved in heated discussions with their family about who was right and who was wrong. They bickered on a daily basis, making the work environment toxic for themselves, their patients, and their employees.

Their partnership lasted less than a year with Melody buying out Lucy's interest. Unfortunately, their lack of communication resulted in a not only a failed partnership, but also a failed friendship and family relationship.

The lesson from Melody's situation is that it is not always the best idea to partner with someone with whom you are emotionally attached. It is common to romanticize the idea of being in business together, but in reality, you must be able to effectively communicate, as well as share complementary value systems for it to work and be a success.

Questions to ponder:

1. Is one partner financially strapped and needing a paycheck every month while the other has saved and is able to put off a paycheck?
2. Does one partner feel like the company checkbook is his or her personal checkbook?
3. Does one partner want a sleek and contemporary office while the other prefers warm and cozy?
4. Does one partner want his or her child to work for the business while the other wants no family involvement?
5. If you are part of the same family, does one of you have a big mouth-- relaying the ins and outs of the business to the entire family while the other one would like to keep business matters private and separate from the family?

Clearly, you have to ask very personal, and sometimes uncomfortable, questions of your prospective partner. Having an open forum for communication will allow the partnership, as well as the business, to last.

"A friendship founded on business is a good deal better than a business founded on friendship."
--John D. Rockefeller, Oil Magnate
& Founder of Standard Oil Company

Buy the Lottery Ticket

A friend of mine heard a story on a popular spiritual radio program that sums up why many of us to do not achieve our goals in life. The story told of a man who prayed year after year to win the lottery. He struggled in his life, went to church and pleaded at the base of a statute to win the lottery. One day, tired of hearing the man's cries, the statute finally answered: "Buy a lottery ticket!"

The moral of the story is, it doesn't matter the magnitude of the step, just take *a* step. Your business will not start itself by simply talking or dreaming about it. You must *do* something. Some of you will take baby steps and others of you will take a "cow jumped over the moon" leap. Some of you will recognize the need for self-evaluation and improvement; while others will feel ready to move forward. Stop procrastinating, making excuses and move forward.

There are many examples of success, but trying to replicate someone else's path to success may not be in your best interest. Do it *your* way. I guarantee you will have challenges but don't let fear block you and naysayers stop you!

To sum up this book, keep these things in mind:

- If you really want a business, don't fall asleep at your 'resting place'.

- Don't confuse passion to start a business with your desire to escape from the discomfort of your career or life.
- Don't automatically assume that your hobby can be the framework for a successful business.
- Apply simple common sense to any business idea that you entertain.
- Be realistic about whatever business you choose to pursue.
- Don't hastily quit your day job to launch your business.
- Don't discount the value of your experience.
- Be a strategic thinker and don't get consumed with minor details.
- Always maintain emotional control when dealing with your employees, venders, and customers.
- Work on your physical, emotional, and spiritual fitness.
- Know your leadership style and make adjustments if appropriate.
- Work on your self-esteem if necessary.
- Don't confuse an inflated ego with assertiveness.
- If you are a more mature prospective entrepreneur, know that you're never too old; but incorporate succession planning early in the business development process.
- Don't expect to launch a successful business if you have been a lazy employee all of your life.
- Understand that just because you are the owner doesn't mean that you will have the biggest paycheck.

- Don't expect a business loan if you have poor credit and no assets.
- Share your dreams for a business with your 'trusted' family and friends.
- When you launch your business, hire expertise instead of 'hacks'.
- You may ultimately feel like a prisoner in a poorly thought out partnership.

Don't expect overnight success, but do expect successes!! Now go get started!

In life and business, there are two cardinal sins. The first is to act precipitously without thought and the second is to not act at all."
-- Carl Icahn, Investor & businessman

About the Author

Beverly Meekins, CPA, CIA has worked in many business and financial disciplines for more than twenty years. She lives in the suburbs of Chicago with her husband and two dogs, Bailey and Blade. She is a certified public accountant and certified internal auditor with an accounting degree from the University of Illinois and a Master of Business Administration from the University of Chicago. She owns The Meekins Group, a CPA and business consulting firm located in the suburbs of Chicago, Illinois (www.themeekinsgroup.com). She also organized The Meekins Institute (www.themeekinsinstitute.org), a non-profit organization that promotes financial literacy. Visit her website at www.beverlymeekins.com or www.bampublishingco.com to learn more about her current and upcoming projects.